The Pathological Liar

*An Essential Guide
to Understanding
Compulsive Lying
Disorder, What Goes on in
the Head of a Pathological
Liar, and How to Get
Them to Stop*

by Debbie Welsch

Table of Contents

Introduction

We've all lied one point or another in our life. Perhaps it was to avoid embarrassment, to avoid hurting a person's feelings, out of sheer convenience, or for another reason with generally innocent intent. However, there are people out there who lie habitually, intentionally deceiving others without remorse. These people are known as "Pathological Liars."

Oftentimes, the tendency to lie is so deeply entrenched in a pathological liar's personality that the lies become interwoven with reality such that even he himself believes them! If you know a person like this, or worse, if you're stuck in a familial or romantic relationship with one, it's only normal for your frustration level to skyrocket on a regular basis when you feel like you're constantly being lied to. In fact, living with a pathological liar can be emotionally dangerous. You can't trust or rely on them, and with such a lack of trust, it's impossible to forge a meaningful, honest, and fruitful relationship.

I'm sure you're wondering by now, "So, can anything be done about this?!?"

Fortunately, the answer is "Yes!" Although it can seem like a gargantuan task, with a little bit of understanding and a lot of effort, it is possible to turn the habitual liar in your life into an honest individual that you can finally trust.

This book is designed to help you understand exactly what compulsive lying disorder is all about, including how pathological liars think in their own minds. And most importantly, it will also provide you with a framework within which you can learn to cope and help force them to stop lying to you altogether. So if this sounds appealing, then let's get started!

Chapter 1: Understanding Compulsive Lying Disorder

Compulsive Lying Disorder is characterized by a blatant disregard for telling the truth and the compulsion to deceive using false statements. The person has a habit of lying, and most of the time, he doesn't acknowledge that he is lying. Often, he finds it difficult to tell the truth. It has not been officially classified as a mental disorder, but psychologists and psychiatrists consider it a unique and special case of mental disorder because it has been observed that there are certain mental factors that affect the behavior of pathological liars.

Causes of Compulsive Lying Disorder

The cause of Compulsive Lying Disorder has not been specifically identified yet, but experts have come up with the following reported causes:

1. Upbringing of the person

It has been observed that children who have grown up in a home that tolerates lying or severely punishes lying are prone to become pathological liars. When children grow up in an environment where lying is a way of life, they think that lying is an approved social behavior. This is also true in children who have been punished severely or traumatized during their childhood that they tend to rebel and lie when they become adults, just to see if they can get away with their actions.

2. Defense mechanism

When people experienced that telling the truth has been predominantly harmful to them, they tend to lie to protect themselves from the pain and humiliation. One example is when parents are abusive; the child tends to lie to give the answer expected from him. Physically and sexually-abused children have the propensity to lie to defend themselves. That's why parents must learn how to appreciate their children when they tell the truth, even if the truth is unpleasant. An example is when a child tells the truth about breaking your favorite vase. Don't force the child to lie because of your expected corporeal punishment. The price of the vase is nothing compared to your child's well-being. You don't want him to turn into a pathological liar, right?

There are also instances in which the person lies because he does not want to recall traumatic events. In this case, telling a lie will serve as his defense mechanism.

Telling the truth must be rewarded instead of you being harsh to the person. When lying becomes a habit of defending one's self, it forms a destructive behavior. Inculcate in the person that unless it's a life threatening situation, people should always opt to be honest.

3. Genetics

Experts observed that pathologic liars usually grew up in a family of liars. This may have something to do with the inheritance of genes responsible for mental health. Some individuals with mental illness or personality disorders are more likely to become compulsive liars. It can also come from the influence of family members on the person's behavior.

4. Mental disorder

In some instances, the person may have a mental disorder that may not be inherited, such as, interdependency, neurological imbalance or conduct disorder. In interdependency, the child is not trained to become independent, and relies on others for his emotional needs. In neurological imbalance, the frontal lobe is impaired, causing mental disorder, while conduct disorder is when a child commits crimes because of the lack of supervision and attention from parents or guardians. The person lies so he can maintain dependency with the other person.

In the Journal of Neuropsychiatry and Clinical Neurosciences, it has been reported that persons with Compulsive Lying Disorders have an impairment on the right hemithalamic part of their brains. Other studies have also reported that the brain of pathological liars have more white matter than the average individual. In this regard, pathological lying appears to be a symptom of a much more complex form of mental disorder.

5. Substances of abuse

Drugs of abuse may also be the cause of compulsive lying. The person deceives other people so that he can respond to his needs for the drug he is addicted to. Examples of substances of abuse are cocaine, heroin, methamphetamine, marijuana and alcohol. The addiction has to be treated first before you can succeed in treating the Compulsive Lying Disorder.

6. Obsession for power

There are narcissists who are obsessed with gaining power because they can exert their control over other people. When they feel that they can control others through this power, they will continue to deceive and spin their lies to hold on to that power. "Absolute power corrupts."

7. Personality disorders

These include behavioral disorders such as, attention deficit hyperactivity disorder (ADHD), antisocial (or dissocial) personality disorder (ASPD), and oppositional defiant disorder (ODD). Traits, such as, selfishness, obsessiveness, possessiveness and being temperamental can lead to compulsive lying. These personality disorders have to be managed and treated before compulsive lying can be cured.

8. Low self-esteem

Some people may lie to boost their self-esteem. They are willing to malign and lie about another person to maintain their public image. When they notice that they can get away with it—it becomes a habit. They will continue to lie blatantly without remorse. Pathological liars are typically anti-social. They don't mind trampling and maligning other people to feed their self-esteem.

The low self-esteem can stem from a lack of education, inferior physical appearance, low academic performance, lack of social status, and/or feelings of insecurity.

In a nutshell, the particular causes mentioned above bring forth the different types of Compulsive Lying Disorder, such as:

- Pathological lying due to substance abuse

- Daydreaming pathological lying

- Pathological lying without apparent reason (habitual lying)

- Pathological lying as an effect of another condition, such as, mental and impulse control disorders

- Pathological lying due to inadequacies (low self-esteem, inferiority complex, low-morale, lack of knowledge, to prevent embarrassment and punishment)

These are the most common causes of Compulsive Lying Disorder. The explicit reasons can vary from one individual to another.

Chapter 2: Identifying the Characteristics of a Pathological Liar

How can you know whether a person is a pathological liar when first meeting him? Well, you can't tell for sure when you're meeting a person for the first time. Hence, you will have to do your own investigation. If it sounds too good to be true, then it's highly probable that the person is lying. Here are characteristics of a pathological liar that you can refer to:

1. **His statements tend to make him appear extraordinary, great or noble.** A person with compulsive lying disorder will exult himself and malign another person so he cannot be faulted. The lie usually favors him.

2. **His lies are not short-lived but continue repeatedly**. He cannot stop, even when it's apparent he's lying through his teeth. He continues to lie and live his life like nothing is wrong.

3. **When confronted with the truth, he will hesitantly accept that his statements were untrue.** When caught red-handed, he may concede that he lied, but he won't feel sorry, and he'll lie again.

4. **His tendency to lie typically comes from within and not an effect of an external factor.** Compulsive liars derive pleasure from lying, and the motivation generally comes from within.

5. **His pronouncements have a shade of fantasy interwoven with some truth.** His lies are products of his imagination, but he uses a grain of truth to make his statements more credible.

6. **He lies without any apparent reason; he just wants to fabricate tales.** It has become a part of his persona. He is addicted to lying. He can't survive a day without lying.

7. **He may be suffering from other mental disorders.** People with mental disorders have

increased risks of lying compulsively. So, double check for any strange behavior.

8. **He may picture himself as a pitiful victim.** Some pathological liars want attention, so they turn themselves into the constant victim of circumstances. An example is when a person lies that his mother had died in a plane crash in order to gain sympathy.

9. **He is inconsistent.** Because of his lies, he contradicts himself often. But this doesn't disconcert him; he just goes on spinning his tales, despite the inconsistencies in his statements.

10. **He has poor self-esteem, feels inferior and feels inadequate.** One of the traits of many compulsive liars is low self-esteem. To boost his self-esteem, he creates his own world of fantasy and make-believe to imagine that he is self-confident and highly-respected.

Therapists or specialists can diagnose the condition by observing these characteristics in a suspected compulsive liar.

Chapter 3: How Compulsive Lying Disorder Is Diagnosed

Diagnosis of Compulsive Lying Disorder is done through various methods. These methods range from simply observing the behavior of the suspected person to performing diagnostic, psychiatric and psychology tests. Lie detector tests won't yield reliable results for pathologic liars because they don't feel any sense of guilt or repentance of their fabrications. Here are the most common techniques:

1. Personal history

The personal history of the individual is evaluated and dishonest episodes are noted. Did he fabricate stories constantly? Did he create a world of lies around him? Did he lie without any twinge of conscience? If the person has displayed any of the traits presented in Chapter 2, and the answer to all these questions are "Yes," then these are determining factors that the individual is a pathological liar.

Any traumatic childhood history must also be included in the evaluation. There are instances in which children who were sexually and physically abused turned to compulsive lying to protect themselves. Dysfunctional families can also be a cause of Compulsive Lying Disorder. History of any of these occurrences can help diagnose the disorder.

2. Electroencephalogram (EEG)

This is a diagnostic procedure which can demonstrate the brain's activity through the use of electrodes. The electrodes are attached to the head, and the waves created by the brain's activity are displayed on a monitor. The result of the suspected person's EGG is then compared to that of a normal test person's EEG. A normal EEG will show these frequencies, expressed in hertz (Hz), with the following bands.

o   Delta – less than 4 Hz

o   Theta – equal or more than 4 Hz but less than 8 Hz

- o Alpha – equal or more than 8 Hz but less than 14 Hz

- o Beta – equal or more than 14 Hz

3. Psychological and psychiatric evaluation for mental disorder

The individual can undertake psychiatric and psychological tests to determine if he has any mental disorder. This can help in diagnosing Compulsive Lying Disorder. Not all people with a mental disorder lie, but some individuals with certain mental impairments become pathological liars because of their distorted misconceptions of what reality is.

The tests can also identify if the person without any mental disorder is a pathological or compulsive liar.

If you want to conduct your own test, here's a simple test you can administer at home to determine if the person is a pathological liar or not:

25

1. Did you ever lie at any time in the past?

   o Always
   o Sometimes
   o Never

2. Do you believe in your own lies?

   o Always
   o Sometimes
   o Never

3. Do you create stories to make yourself appear good?

   o Always
   o Sometimes
   o Never

4. Do you lie to gain sympathy?

    o Always
    o Sometimes
    o Never

5. Has anyone ever accused you of lying?

    o Always
    o Sometimes
    o Never

6. Do you feel the compulsion to lie?

    o Always
    o Sometimes
    o Never

7. Do you lie to others so you can appear confident?

- o Always
- o Sometimes
- o Never

8. Do you feel uneasy when others confront you with the truth?

- o Always
- o Sometimes
- o Never

9. Do you lie even when people can easily check the veracity of your statements?

- o Always
- o Sometimes
- o Never

10. Do you feel uneasy telling the truth?

- o Always
- o Sometimes
- o Never

Score your answers based on these points: Always = 5 points; Sometimes = 3; Never = 0

Interpretation:

0 to 3 – Congratulations, you're definitely not a pathological liar!

6 to 19 – Oops, Watch out! You're now on your way of becoming a pathological liar. Be conscious of your statements and avoid telling lies.

22 to 37 – You're on the verge of turning into a pathological liar. Determine the reasons why you lie and solve the root causes.

40 and above—You're a pathological liar. You have to acknowledge this so that you can do something about your compulsive lying before things get worse.

4. Polygraph test

This is also called the "Lie Detector" test. It measures the physiologic responses of the body to the declarations of the person taking the test. These physiologic reactions include the pulse rate (PR), respiration, blood pressure and skin conductivity. When a person lies, these vital signs are typically increased. However, there are documented cases of pathological liars beating the polygraph test because lying is already "normal" for them, so there won't be any abnormal physiologic responses. Some compulsive liars also have the ability to manipulate the results the way they want to.

5. Verbal and nonverbal signs

The person's verbal and nonverbal language must also be observed for symptoms of lying.

Here are some verbal and nonverbal signs that may indicate that the person is lying:

- o Profuse sweating

- o Fidgeting

- o Clearing throat

- o Brushing hair

- o Incongruent verbal and nonverbal cues – he smiles when stating a sad story

- o Placing an object between the person he's talking to

- o Blinking often

- o Adjusting tie

- o Shifting weight

- o Licking or biting of the lips

- o Turning away from the person he's talking to

- o Short responses

- o Phony smile – when he smiles, the smile doesn't reach his eyes

- o Using qualifiers often such as, "usually" and "basically" when speaking

Again, if the pathological liar is aware of these cues, he will try his best not to do them so his lies won't be detected. You will have to be smarter than he is by utilizing all possible methods to confirm your suspicion.

At present, there are no specific diagnostic laboratory tests to detect Compulsive Lying Disorder.

Chapter 4: What Goes on in the Head of a Pathological Liar

A pathological liar exists in his own make-believe world and weaves his own lies to achieve his fantasies. There are a number of reasons why pathological liars lie. What goes on in their heads when they fabricate statements?

Pathological liar due to drug abuse

This type of liar has difficulty controlling his drug addiction; he has to buy the drug no matter what. So, he will think of ways to satiate his desire for the substance of abuse. He lies to ask for money or he lies to hide his addiction and he becomes dishonest so he can procure the drug. His addiction to the drug forces him to lie. His thoughts can be:

- "I've got to lie to mom that I'll pay my tuition fee, so I can buy heroin."

- "I have to lie where I went to avoid the discovery of my addiction."

- "I'll hang out with my friends for some crack, but I won't tell my parents."

Daydreaming pathological liar

The thoughts of this type of pathological liar are of grandeur and fantasy in which the liar plays the role of the hero or heroine. He creates myths in his mind and lives in them, daydreaming in his own world of lies. Here are some examples:

- "I'm the son of a wealthy business tycoon and I have three cars and a jet."

- "My parents are both in the entertainment industry, but I don't want to reveal their true identities because fans and reporters might harass me."

- "My residence is in Beverly Hills, right next to various celebrities. In fact, I might be entering showbiz very soon."

When you observe the person's lifestyle and behavior, these statements are highly improbable, and you will notice that his statements are exaggerated and seem too good to be true.

Pathological lying without apparent reason (habitual lying)

A pathological liar can lie without any reason. He thinks that his lies are the truth and thinks that facts are not worth revealing. He feels uncomfortable when telling the truth.

- "I don't want to tell the truth."

- "Telling a lie is more fun."

- "I'm happy deceiving people."

Pathological lying as an effect of another condition such as, mental and impulse control disorders

In this case, his mind is not sane, so he lies because of his underlying disorder. He thinks differently to the average normal person because his brain is impaired.

- "I'm not sure; I think this is the truth."

- "My mind is confused. I'll say whatever comes to my mind."

Pathological lying due to inadequacies

His thoughts are full of self-doubt, fear, anxiety and inadequacies. He thinks he's inferior to others, that they're smarter and more good-looking or self-confident than him. He feels that he's not loved, accepted, or admired. He imagines himself with all the virtues he lacks and lies to let people believe he has these virtues.

- "Nobody should know that I can't speak well. I'll skip class reporting and tell them I have been sick."

- "I have to lie and tell them that I graduated valedictorian from high school, so that they'll admire me."

- "I have to lie and tell them that I come from a rich family, so that they will accept me readily into their group."

These are the thoughts that run through the minds of the most common types of pathological liars. You must learn how they think so you can cope with these behaviors effectively.

Chapter 5: How to Get a Pathologic Liar to Stop Lying

Getting pathologic liars to stop lying is a Herculean task, unless the person has the desire to change. In addition, the person must be self-motivated to change and become an honest person. Here are simple steps that you can follow:

Step #1 – Have a heart-to-heart talk with the person

Talk to the concerned person and explain that his constant lying is causing problems within the family and the people around him. Choose a quiet and private area where people cannot intrude. His room may be the best option. There should be no distractions; turn off TVs and radios. Talk to him in a calm and collected manner and never shout or be offensive. You have to convince him that something is wrong with him, and that before change can happen, he has first to acknowledge his wrongdoing.

Once you have convinced him to acknowledge this, allow him to evaluate his own actions. This can be more productive than you passing judgment on his actions. You can use the questions in Chapter 3 to determine how serious his lying behavior is. Afterwards, let him write down his lies on a sheet of paper and next to these lies the resulting negative effect. Afterwards, let him recommend the steps that can correct the negative effects. Of course, the answer would be: to stop telling lies. Hence, let him participate actively in the formulation of his primary goal—that is to stop lying.

Teaching kids about honesty must start from within the family. Parents and members of the family must show to their children that "honesty *is* the best policy" through their own actions. Kids have a keen sense of intuition. They know immediately whether you're above board or not. Talking to children about the importance of honesty and being a role model is the best way parents can teach their children. Sanctioning children using corporal punishment the first time he lies is only going to give him a traumatic experience that can create enmity. Instead of obeying the parent, the child may rebel and carry on with his lies.

He must first accept his wrongdoing and be self-motivated to change before you can proceed with Step #3. You can use Step #2 to help convince him.

Step #2 – Consult a specialist or therapist on Compulsive Lying Disorder

If you want to confirm your suspicions, you can consult a specialist. Consulting a specialist or therapist will also ensure that the person is monitored properly. The specialist will conduct tests and can monitor the pathological liar's progress. Consequently, you have to implement whatever recommendations the specialist suggests. If the liar is in self-denial, the specialist can help you convince him.

Step #3 – Inform members of the family discreetly

Whether you consult a specialist or not, you have to inform family members and people who are within the vicinity of the pathological liar about the plan.

This is vital because family members will act as observers and can lend moral support to the pathological liar's quest for change.

Step #4 – Keep a logbook to record the pathological liar's progress

Record all his lies from thereon. Specify the dates, the circumstances in which the lie was said, to whom the lie was directed and the specific statement spoken. Do this on a daily basis. At the end of the day, go over the logbook with him and let him know about his progress. You will act as his "captain"; you guide his actions in the correct direction, but he has to "steer the wheel." Discuss each incident where he lied and ask him why he did it. Based on the reasons, address the problem by solving the issues. Always remind him of his goal – not to lie.

Step #5 – Reward honest behavior

This is a way to motivate him more, especially if he is a child. The rewards need not be material things. This can be a word of appreciation or praise, such as, "Good job", "You're finally getting there," or "That was cool." A trip to his favorite ice cream parlor or a trip to the zoo will also do, as long as these are worthwhile activities that can increase your bond with the compulsive liar.

Step #6 – Teach by example

You can never teach a pathological liar to be honest if you don't serve as a role model. Be honest through your actions and words, and you can be a reliable and credible guide for him in telling the truth. People around him should likewise show honesty in their dealings with him.

Step #7 – Practice, practice and practice

Telling the truth can be difficult for people who have told lies often. So, you can provide him a venue where he can practice. Family members, friends or trusted individuals can help as the questioner and listener while the liar practices how to speak the truth.

These are the simple steps you can implement. You have to be persistent. Change cannot happen overnight. You have to keep repeating these steps until they become effective for him.

Chapter 6: Treatments for Compulsive Lying Disorder

There are certain interventions for Compulsive Lying Disorder that are usually done by mental health specialists in this area. These interventions are individualized because no two persons are exactly alike.

1. Cognitive Behavior Therapy

The mental health specialist will conduct behavior modification of the pathological liar through weekly therapy sessions; the specialist interacts with the person and talks to him. The specialist will help the liar substitute positive thoughts in place of negative ones. Then the specialist assigns homework to the pathological liar or things to do until the next session.

2. Drug medications

When the Compulsive Lying Disorder is caused by personality disorders, antidepressants, antipsychotic and anxiolytic (anti-anxiety) drugs are given to treat the underlying condition. By treating the underlying condition, pathological lying can also be eradicated.

Here are some examples of antidepressants:

o **MAOIs (monoamine oxidase inhibitors)** – Isocarboxazid and Selegiline

   Side effects – headaches, weight gain and nausea

o **SSRIs (selective serotonin reuptake inhibitors)** – Citalopram, Fluoxetine, Sertraline

Side effects – dizziness, nausea, diarrhea, weight problems, drowsiness and tremors

o **Tricyclic antidepressants** – the most common being Doxepin, Trimipramine, Imipramine and Clomipramine

Side effects – constipation, loss of sex drive, disorientation, dry mouth and tachycardia (increased heartbeat)

Here are some examples of antipsychotic drugs:

o **Clozapine**—Clozaril

Side effects – agranulocytosis (loss of blood cells, agranulocytes that contributes to the defense mechanism of the body. This can make the person susceptible to any infection.)

o **Risperidone**—Risperdal

Side effects – drowsiness, insomnia, headache, orthostatic hypotension (drop in blood pressure when the person tries to stand)

<u>Here are some examples of anxiolytic drugs</u> (these drugs can cause addiction and serious reactions in the body that are life threatening, so they must only be used under the supervision of a licensed doctor.):

o **Benzodiazepines** – Diazepam, Xanax, Tranxene and Librium

Side effects – can cause addiction to the drug, drowsiness, hypotension (low blood pressure), muscle weakness, urinary retention, fatigue and incontinence (inability to control urination and defecation)

o **Barbiturates** – Seconal, Nembutal and Mebaral

Side effects – addiction, possible seizures upon withdrawal of the drug, symptoms of Central Nervous System (CNS) depression, such as, drowsiness, lack of muscle coordination, and weakened muscles

In addition, you have to be certain that the person is not allergic to any of the components of these medications. Severe anaphylactic reactions can cause death.

3. Psychotherapy

This is another option for treatment if the cause of the Compulsive Lying Disorder is an antisocial behavior. With this method, the pathological liar is subjected to therapy sessions with a psychologist based on his individual evaluation. It's also a process of mental conditioning to help the person come

to terms with his dishonesty and become a
better person.

Take note that treatments using behavioral
interventions are highly individualized, so you have to
visit a mental health specialist on a regular basis.

If the pathological liar has no mental disorder,
Cognitive Behavioral Therapy and psychotherapy –
without medications – may be sufficient in treating
the pathological liar.

Chapter 7: Additional Tips for Coping with a Pathological Liar

When coping with pathological liars, you have to remember that there are numerous reasons why they lie. Get to the bottom of those lies and you're halfway to achieving your goal. To guide you more in doing this, here are some tips you can use:

1. **At first, the pathological liar may be in self-denial.** This is normal. You have to be persistent in showing him that he has a problem. Document his statements to prove your point. Once he accepts his wrongdoing, change can come more easily.

2. **Treatment can only succeed if the compulsive liar is self-motivated.** This is crucial to the success of any intervention. It's because the person will monitor himself without constant prodding.

3. **Allow the pathological liar to practice telling the truth.** Lying is second nature to him, so he has to practice telling the truth. Have a chat with him and allow him to exercise honest behavior.

4. **Forcing a pathological liar to undergo treatment can inflict more harm**. That's why the "acknowledgment phase" is important when you want to treat a compulsive liar. When you force treatment, he may become defensive and lie all the more.

5. **Most pathological liars lack sympathy**. He may not feel guilty about lying to you because he simply doesn't understand the reason for telling the truth; even if he does know, he doesn't believe in it.

6. **Pathological liars can consciously change their body language**. Nonverbal cues do not always accurately reveal whether a person is lying or not. Keep in mind that compulsive liars can manipulate the way they talk and act.

7. **In the diagnosis of Compulsive Lying Disorder, all data must be integrated.** The traits, lab test results (if any), behavior and psychological or psychiatric tests must all be considered. Normal people do lie, so be careful when labeling people as pathological liars.

8. **Compulsive Lying Disorder has no official classification.** To date, the condition has not yet been officially classified as a chronic mental disorder. Psychologists and psychiatrists have differing opinions. But definitely, there's something wrong with how pathological liars think.

9. **Pathological liars can tell the truth, but in a distorted way.** You must be aware of this fact so you can sift the information being given to you. Asking the person clarifying questions can help unravel the genuine truth.

10. **Don't reveal any emotions when talking to a compulsive liar.** When he observes you reacting to his lies; he becomes more enthused in continuing to dish out his fabrications.

11. **Surround the compulsive liar with an environment of honesty.** When what he sees around him are actions of honesty, he's encouraged to do likewise. It has to come from within for him to finally get rid of his habitual lies.

12. **Let the person feel that despite his deception, you still love him**. Despise the action but not the person. Tell him that you're not happy with his actions but you still love him. This positive behavior will make him feel more secure and motivated to change for the better.

Use these tips when dealing with compulsive or pathological liars. The essential thing to remember is that not all pathological liars behave the same way; you have to deal with the specific behavior of the individual pathological liar.

Conclusion

Stopping a pathological or compulsive liar from telling lies involves a complex set of strategies. You will have to pick the methods applicable to the individual you're trying to motivate. For you to succeed, you have to first get the person to acknowledge his fault and be self-motivated to change. Only then can you start effective treatment. You also have to determine the reasons why he lies.

It has been discovered that some pathological liars have certain mental disorders. This has to be determined before treatment is initiated. In cases like these, the mental disorder has to be treated first to eliminate the cause. When this is accomplished, the treatment of the disorder itself will be less complicated.

Your success in this endeavor will depend on your persistence and communication skills. You must keep trying to let the pathological liar understand the negative effects of his actions. You have to let him realize the enormous benefits he can reap from being honest. Because, as the cliché goes: "Honesty *is* the best policy."

Finally, I'd like to thank you for purchasing this book! If you enjoyed it or found it helpful, I'd greatly appreciate it if you'd take a moment to leave a review on Amazon. Thank you!

Printed in Great Britain
by Amazon

43371687R00040